KT-394-759

Vis-Ability

Raising Awareness of Vision Impairment

Vicki L Griggs

Copyright © 2020 Vicki L Griggs

The moral right of the author has been asserted.

Apart from any fair dealing for the purposes of research or private study, or criticism or review, as permitted under the Copyright, Designs and Patents Act 1988, this publication may only be reproduced, stored or transmitted, in any form or by any means, with the prior permission in writing of the publishers, or in the case of reprographic reproduction in accordance with the terms of licences issued by the Copyright Licensing Agency. Enquiries concerning reproduction outside those terms should be sent to the publishers.

Matador
9 Priory Business Park,
Wistow Road, Kibworth Beauchamp,
Leicestershire. LE8 0RX
Tel: 0116 279 2299
Email: books@troubador.co.uk
Web: www.troubador.co.uk/matador
Twitter: @matadorbooks

ISBN 978 183859 209 7

British Library Cataloguing in Publication Data.
A catalogue record for this book is available from the British Library.

Printed and bound by CPI Group (UK) Ltd, Croydon, CR0 4YY
Typeset in 16pt Minion Pro by Troubador Publishing Ltd, Leicester, UK

Matador is an imprint of Troubador Publishing Ltd

MIX
Paper from
responsible sources
FSC
www.fsc.org
FSC® C013604

I dedicate this book to my mum.

Thanks, Mum, for being my rock in
life, for being my voice, for always
having faith in me and for all your help
in getting me where I want to be.
We have been through a lot together.
Luv u loads, Muma xxxx

In loving memory of
my lovely grandparents,

Grandma and Grandad Griggs

and

Grandma and Grandad Seeley

and

my great aunty Edna.

You are all missed every day xxxx

Contents

About Me

I live in a lovely little village in Hertfordshire with my mum and dad along with our furry and feathered family: Bertie and Jessie (our two dogs), and Sunny (my baby Senegal parrot). Bertie is a Yorkshire Terrier and although he is a small dog, he has loads of energy, so loves long walks. Jessie is our manic but lovely Labrador x collie, who enjoys making you hold her bone for her to chew on! Sunny is like a little monkey acrobat and delights in showing off (especially when Mum is eating grapes and he wants one!). I also have an older brother, Wayne, who lives a five-minute car ride away from us.

In my spare time, I love spending time with my family and pets, playing table tennis, dancing, going to the theatre, reading and doing anything to do with Potter.

The aim of this book is not only to raise awareness of vision impairment, but also to reach out to those who have a vision impairment.

This is my story about my own experiences of having a vision impairment and will give you factual information on this subject too. If this book helps just one person, then I have achieved my goal.

Hope you find it useful!

South Dublin Libraries

www.southdublinlibraries.ie

WHAT IS VISION IMPAIRMENT AND FEVR?

When Things Get Tough

"Things are going smoothly,
And life is great,
Then something happens,
Turns your life upside down,
Thrown in at the deep end,
Not knowing what is happening,
Just living each day as it comes.

Life is like a rollercoaster,
With so many ups and downs
along the way,
You're worried and scared and
angry.

With all these emotions running
through you,
You don't know just what to do,
Putting on a brave face,
To just carry on.
Being brave, strong and positive,
To just get through it,
Then you fall down,
Hit a brick wall,
Feel you're being weak,
Letting people down,
'Cause all you wanna do is,
Hide, give up, let the darkness
swallow you up.

*You somehow find the strength
within you,
To pull yourself back up,
Brush yourself down.
Being brave, strong and positive,
Is how you get through it,
Always be grateful for the things
you've got,
Family, friends, people who
support you,
You have no idea when things
might change.
When things get tough,
Think to yourself,
I can get through this."*

By Vicki Griggs

Vision impairment is a visual disability where a person has any sort of vision loss that cannot be corrected to a normal level by using glasses or contact lenses, etc.

Some people can only see centrally (tunnel vision), which can be caused by damage to the optic nerve or retina at the back of the eye. Others can only see peripherally, which means they cannot see centrally, but around the outside of things. This is usually found in people that have age-related wet or dry macular degeneration but can also affect younger people who may have an eye disease or condition that affects the retina.

Some people can only see with blurry or misty vision. This can be caused by having a cataract or being short-sighted.

I am short-sighted and only have vision in one eye. Being short-sighted means that I can see things close up but distant objects appear blurred or fuzzy. When I am out and about, I wear glasses to help, but even with glasses my distance vision is still blurry.

FEVR

All my life my parents have called it the 'Vicki Griggs Syndrome', but now it is actually nice to know exactly what it is, to be able to put a name to it and to know what the disease might entail.

There are many types of eye diseases and conditions. My eye condition is very rare; it is called FEVR (familial exudative vitreoretinopathy), which, in a roundabout way, means I have a genetic eye disease involving the blood vessels and retina at the back of the eye. What's strange is that none of my family have any trace of it. As a disease, it cannot be treated, but the symptoms can be.

Symptoms of FEVR are:

» Retinal detachment – loss of vision (although if caught early enough, some vision can be saved).
» Flashes of light and floaters.
» Glaucoma – high pressure in the eye (causing pain), can cause sight loss if not treated.
» Vitreous detachment (also known as posterior vitreous detachment or PVD). The jelly

part of the eye comes away from the retinal wall and this can cause floaters and flashing lights.
» Abnormal blood vessels – these can cause fluid leakage and bleeding into the eye.

Sometimes I feel really angry and resentful, as I am the only member of my family who has this disease and would like to know why I am the odd one out.

THE EARLY YEARS AND MY PROSTHETIC EYE

I was born three weeks premature. Within hours of being born I gave my mum a scare; she was trying to feed me when I turned blue. I was rushed off to special care, where I stayed for ten days.

I was a rather difficult baby. I didn't sleep through the night until I was eighteen months old. Mum would pick me up and cuddle me until I was asleep, then lay me down in my cot where I would open one eye and start crying again.

I was born with a squint in my right eye (a lazy eye), which wandered inwards; so, at the age of one year, I had a squint correction and an examination under anaesthetic (EUA). At the age of four, I was laying on the floor colouring when I said to Mum, "My eye has gone all funny." I didn't say any more about it, but when she tested my right eye a bit later, by covering my left eye and holding up her fingers, I could not see.

Fortunately, we were going to Moorfields the next day, having been referred by the optician.

At Moorfields, we met Mr Aylward, who was to be my consultant for the next eighteen years. Clumps of abnormal blood vessels were discovered in both of my eyes. The abnormal blood vessels in my right eye had bled into the vitreous (the jelly part of the eye). They said to leave it a few weeks to see if it would clear on its own, but it didn't. I had a vitrectomy under general anaesthetic; this removed the jelly which contained the blood.

A few months later, my retina detached in my right eye, so I had to have it repaired under general anaesthetic. My memories of that time are good, as Mum tried to make it as fun as possible. I had a bag of presents to open from a friend whilst in hospital and when it was bath time, I had these Tiny Tots toys that squirted water if I filled them up and squeezed them. I found it rather funny to squirt Mum and make her all wet.

The only thing that left an emotional scar on me at that time was the smell of the dressing that they put over my hand with the numbing cream. Whenever I thought about those times in hospital, the smell of the dressing would return and it would make me shudder, and still does. Also, I went off pizza for years as I had pizza in hospital and hated it.

The question I have always asked myself is, why hadn't these abnormal blood vessels in my eyes been discovered when I had the EUA at the age of one? Could some of my future problems have been prevented? The sad thing is that before all this, I was quite a happy, confident child and was where I should be with my development, etc. That changed. I don't know if it was to do with the two operations I had, or leaving pre-school (where my mum was pre-school leader at the time) to start primary school, or my best friend leaving the school, or if it was all three things combined, but I lost all my confidence and fell behind my peer group.

Another theory that I have is that it wasn't correctly understood how much I could actually see. I was up with my peer group in pre-school due to the fact that there was no board work, therefore it would not have been picked up that I couldn't see. I fell behind my peer group when I started school, because board work was introduced and it hadn't been realised that I needed that bit of extra help in completing class work.

The operation that I had at the age of one had made my eye wander outwards instead of inwards. I had to patch my right eye to make it work, as it was a lazy eye (squint). I really hated this, because it involved putting a patch on my good eye as the other had reduced vision. Mum used to make sure we were doing something to distract me from the fact that I had the patch on. She tried different tactics with me, from putting a patch on my toy car Bessie to making a scrapbook of all my patches. For every seven patches (one patch a day) I would get a little present at the end of the week, and for each patch I could choose a special animal sticker to put on it.

When I started primary school, I didn't want to go because I wouldn't be with

Mum, so she said that if I was good and went to school, at the end of the week I could get a guinea pig. I did go to school and got my guinea pig, 'Pickle'. He was my little friend and I loved him very much.

I started going to ballet lessons when I was two years old but gave up when I was five or six. Then, when I was eight, I started disco dancing.

Everything was then stable with my eyes until I was twelve, when I had another squint operation done on my right eye to straighten it as it often wandered out. I would never see it looking straight in the mirror and would always believe that it was never straight even when my parents used to say it was. I had quite a black eye after that operation. I will never forget that feeling, though, when I looked into the mirror after having the squint operation and saw my right eye straight for the very first time. I ignored the bruising that was around my eye and exclaimed, "WICKED!"

In 2001, an animal sanctuary called EASE opened in our village. I adopted (sponsored) one of the New Forest foals, Amber. I became their youngest volunteer and would go over every Saturday no matter what the weather. I became rather attached to a certain Shetland pony called Bumble, whom I would spend the most time with. I was devastated when the sanctuary closed in 2005.

Just ten days before my fourteenth birthday, I had to make the most difficult decision I have ever had to make… to have my right eye removed and to have an implant and prosthetic eye in its place. The retina had detached at the back of my eye and started bleeding, eventually leaving it permanently stained red/green, painfully sore and very light sensitive (especially when out in the sun, where I would walk with my head down as both eyes became watery) and it left me very ill. I wasn't eating, as everything tasted horrible.

From March to August 2003, I had flare-ups of bleeding in my eye, turning it green, leaving me in severe pain and bed bound. These would last up to twenty-four to forty-eight hours but would take my eye about a week for the blood to clear in my eye.

No one could say why it had suddenly started to bleed. Mum thought that the squint operation the year before might have upset it and made it bleed. Even if that were true, I have never regretted having the squint operation, as the memory of that moment when I first looked in the mirror and saw it straight for the first time is something that I will treasure always.

I had to have hourly drops when the pain in my eye was severe and then reduced them to three times a day. Mum would have to come in to school at lunchtime to do my drops for me.

One memory I have is when school started back in September 2003. I had a Moorfields appointment in the afternoon and I was determined to go into school for the morning to do my planner (fill in my lessons timetable), but I wasn't really well enough to be there. After writing just a few words, I had my head on the table with my eyes closed. That afternoon I was admitted to the children's ward at Moorfields. Mum had literally carried me up the road to the hospital from the station. I was very weak through not eating and in extreme pain. There was talk of an operation the following day, but I wasn't having that. I got up the next morning and went down to the 'Friends of Moorfields' shop and got a magazine and then back up to the ward and did some drawing. Later they discharged me.

The following week we were back at Moorfields, and again Mum virtually carried me up the road to the hospital. Well, you have probably worked out what happened next... I was admitted a second time. The pressure in my right eye was more than twice what it should have been. An operation to reduce the pressure was discussed and I was taken into a side room to have bloods done, but I completely freaked out and fainted.

I had to have the operation and was put in a wheelchair as my legs had gone shaky. The morning of the operation, I could feel Mum leaning over me in bed, but I was grumpy and wanted to be left alone and told her to go away. Sorry, Mum. Also, I remember her bribing me to eat a sandwich for dinner and saying I could watch *EastEnders* if I got up to have it.

I will never forget the first time it was suggested that my best option was to have my right eye removed. Mum was talking to my consultant, Mr Aylward, while I stayed in the waiting area listening to my Walkman. I am an S Club 7 fan and was listening to one of their songs, 'Bring It All Back', and the words really spoke to me, as it was about life not being easy, that things happen to us for a reason and through the hard times not to forget who we are and never to give up.

I would lay in bed listening to *Harry Potter* tapes, but I spent most of my time asleep, because if I was asleep, then I wasn't in pain. I had many late-night discussions with Mum about having the implant and prosthetic eye.

At first, I was adamant that I wasn't having it done and it took me eight torturous months to make the final decision of having my right eye removed. You can imagine what it was like for Mum and Dad watching me suffer and struggling to make that decision.

When talking about my implant/prosthesis, it was always referred to as 'IT', because using the proper name would make it a real thing, which I was scared of.

> *"Fear of a name increases fear of the thing itself."*
> **Professor Albus Dumbledore**
> *(JK Rowling, 1997, p.216)*

The questions I wanted to be answered about the prosthesis were:

Q: Will it move with my other
      eye?

A: *It will make slight movements*
      with the other eye. I have had
      to train myself not to make
      big movements to the left or
      right as it gets left behind and
      looks weird.

When the anaesthetist came to see me
before I had the eye removed, he told me
the prosthetic eye would not move at all,
which made me freak out and they had
to get the consultant to come and talk to
me to calm me down, but the anaesthetist
had got it wrong.

Q: When I cry, will I still have
      tears?

A: *It will still produce tears.*

(More tears than the other eye, and the tears are warmer.)

Q: Will the eyelid always be puffy? (I had seen a picture of someone else's prosthetic eye.)

A: *Depends on how tired you are at any time. I could have had an injection/treatment to reduce the puffiness but chose not to.*

After the operation, I had a pressure bandage over my eye to reduce the swelling and give it time to heal. When I had that removed, a clear shell was inserted into the socket to ensure the eye kept its shape. Mum decorated some black patches with sequins so when out and about I could keep it covered.

I was referred to the prosthetics team at Moorfields to design me a prosthetic eye to match my other eye and was given a temporary prosthesis that came the nearest to matching my other eye colour until my one was made.

To get the mould of the socket of the eye, they have to put moulding liquid into the socket and wait a few minutes for it to set before removing it. Then they can get to work on matching the details of the colours in your remaining eye.

The detailed work that is put into making the prosthesis is incredible. They use really thin thread for creating the effect of blood vessels of the eye and the colours are carefully painted.

One weekend, when I was still wearing the clear shell, we were sat watching a movie when I accidentally knocked the shell and it came out. We didn't know how to put it back in so we ended up having to go to A&E at Moorfields to get it re-inserted!

Those three times that I was admitted on the children's ward, I was not under the care of Mr Aylward, but on all three occasions he very kindly managed to come and visit me (due to the fact that he had bumped into Mum and Dad around the hospital following my admissions).

Ever since my right eye turned green and then when I lost the eye, my self-confidence abandoned me; I didn't think I was normal any more. My self-image changed forever as I had lost a part of me, never to be the same again.

I still don't think I look normal now, but when other people look at me, they don't realise I have lost an eye... but I know.

Sometimes it hits me just as hard as when I first lost it, even more so when I have to take out the prosthesis to clean it. If I take too long, a feeling of realisation and grief can overwhelm me. I don't think you ever fully recover, as there are constant reminders. That is partly why I don't clean it as often as I should, but also because I am rather forgetful.

If you are a fan of *Harry Potter*, you will know of Mad-Eye Moody, the new Defence Against the Dark Arts teacher in *Goblet of Fire*. (Don't freak out, prosthetic eyes **don't** look anything like Mad-Eye Moody's!) He has a magical eye that swivels around, can see through walls and can be taken out. Well, mine does all of those things (well, not the seeing through walls bit, although I wish it could!). No; what I mean is that I can take mine out too. It can also swivel around in the socket if I rub my eye too hard. I am still quite self-conscious of it swivelling when I rub my eye, because it can look like a lazy eye going inwards or outwards; although most of the time I can feel when I have knocked it.

I have to have scans/pictures taken of my left eye when I go for my reviews and, sometimes, they have gone to try and take a picture of my right eye too. I have had to tell them I have a prosthetic right eye and that has left them a little embarrassed. I have been quite tempted to play a prank on them and to let them take the picture and see their reaction when the scan shows nothing; but I think that would be too mean… maybe one day.

I feel I was deprived of my teen years, as I spent my early teens ill with my right eye and then much of the rest of the time was spent trying to accept the loss of my eye and in trying to rebuild my confidence. I feel that I missed out on many things other teenagers would do. I couldn't go to sleepovers when my eye was bad, as I needed drops so many times a day.

THE EDUCATION SYSTEM

Trying to get the teachers at school to understand my eye condition was difficult. I could not copy from the board, because looking up and down made me lose my place and I would end up writing the same sentence again. If I left my glasses at home, I wouldn't be able to see a thing, so I would have to copy from a friend sitting next to me. I did not have the confidence to tell my teacher.

It was a bit better when they began giving me handouts of what was on the board, but that only happened in certain lessons.

They assumed that vision impairment meant I could not see close up but being short-sighted meant I could. They enlarged the sheets for me, which would have been great for someone who needed them, but I didn't and felt it brought unnecessary attention to my problem, as the sheets would cover the whole table.

In primary school, 'telly time' was a big problem, as I had to sit at the front to be able to see and, like at home, I would sit very close and some of my peers would make it difficult for me, as they thought I was pushing in. I think if the teachers had explained that I needed to sit at the front it might have made things a lot easier.

Throughout my education, Mum had numerous meetings with the teachers, but she never got very far. She was fighting the system to help me, because I didn't have the confidence to speak up for myself; she was my voice. I feel very lucky to have a mum that cares so much, because she has been my rock through thick and thin. It's fair to say that if it hadn't been for Mum getting revision books and going over and over things with me, I would not have got the results I achieved in my GCSEs and certainly would not have got to where I am today. She spent hours sitting with me at home going through homework and revision because, what with not being able to copy from the board and being slow at writing and most of the time not understanding what I was meant to be doing, I didn't get much class work done.

I tried my hardest at school but felt very let down, especially at secondary school. I wanted to learn but found myself in the bottom sets with kids that messed around and misbehaved. It seemed to me that if I had been naughty and disruptive, I would have received more help, but because I kept my head down and tried to get on with it, I struggled.

It was only when I did Animal Care Level 1 at Oaklands College as part of my vocational option for my GCSEs that the tutors had the knowledge and understanding that I needed that bit of extra help. Thank you!

At the end of year ten, because I was so unhappy, Mum and Dad arranged a meeting with my teachers. They had decided to take me out of school and to teach me from home. They asked me to write down exactly how I felt in a statement to take with them and here it is:

July 2005

"I HATE school!

I am fed up with everything.

Since September, I have really struggled to cope. Everything has changed. I came back to school after having my eye removed and went straight into coursework and exams. We were told I would be able to go to the support centre, as I had a lot of time off, but nothing happened. I found it hard to settle back in and really struggled.

A few weeks into term, my best friend abandoned me and my other friends gave me a hard time as well. I had no one to turn to except Mum and Jody, my art therapist. I was really unhappy and still am. I feel that everyone at school is giving up on me and leaving me to struggle alone.

I don't like going to school. I want to be taught at home, because I feel that I don't learn much at school. For my exams, I think I would have failed everything had it not been for Mum teaching me from the books we bought ourselves.

I am still having to copy from the

board, which I can't do even sitting at the front of the class. I sometimes strain my eye trying to read from the board and this is tiring and frustrating, so I sometimes just sit there and do nothing.

I am not confident enough to ask for copies of work. I am trying to be more confident but get frustrated with myself because I'm not.

I have the card to give to teachers, but in one lesson the teacher just looked at the first line and gave it back to me without reading it all and in other lessons when I have handed it in, they start off giving me copies of the work or writing it down for me, but then after a few lessons they stop.

V. Griggs"

The school said to trial a couple of weeks into the new school term, as it was my GCSE year and quite an important stage of my education. I agreed to the trial run and stayed until I finished in May 2006.

I looked forward to the school prom in late May 2006. Mum gave two friends and me a lift there. At the end of the night, I couldn't find my two friends that I went with, as everyone had formed a big circle for the finale song, 'New York, New York'. I tried to break into the circle so that I could join in, but no one would let me in, so I ended up outside of the circle watching everyone else. The teaching staff present did not even notice what was going on! My friends had left without saying goodbye to me. When Mum came and got me, I burst into tears as I was so upset.

Mum contacted the mother of two children who had been taught from home. The eldest had set up a drama group for teenagers and asked if I would be interested in joining. I did join and became a bit more confident. I had a monologue to say and when it came time to perform, I was shaking like a leaf; but I ignored all of that and said it loudly and clearly and was rather pleased with myself.

Unfortunately, I couldn't keep going for as long as I wanted because it was my GCSE year and revision took all my time.

My advice to all schools/teachers is that if you have a student who has a vision impairment or any other disability, don't make them feel the way I felt at school. Talk to them and their parents about what the school can do to help with school work, etc; this will not necessarily be what the school thinks the child needs.

If teachers don't understand the disability themselves, look it up and make sure all staff members are aware of the problem.

Talk to the class as a whole about the disability, letting them freely ask questions about it and ask the child in question if they wish to be present to talk to the class about their disability. (Maybe bring the topic into a PSHE lesson.)

Read the book *Wonder* by RJ Palacio to the class in primary school, and maybe study the book in English lessons if in secondary school, to get the class to understand that it is not what you look like that determines who you are.

If parents say that their child is struggling with school work and needs a copy of the work that is on the board, listen to them and do something about it.

Schools can help by providing support for the close friends of the individual that is going through trauma too.

I would like to thank Mrs Campbell (Class 4 teacher at primary school) and Mrs Coyston (form tutor at secondary school), who did their best to help me.

BULLYING

I, like many children, was bullied at school. Although it was mostly verbal bullying, it did have a major effect on me socially and emotionally.

In primary school, there was a girl who was jealous of me and she would try to be friends with my best friends. She would say to my best friend, "I want a private word with you," in front of me and they would walk off together around the playground and leave me on my own. It made me think they were talking about me behind my back. She would also hide my things too so that I couldn't find them!

I thought I had a good group of friends at secondary school, but when I went back after my 'big op', they all turned on me when I needed them the most. My best friend did not want to be friends anymore; I couldn't understand what I had done, although she said it was her not me, and that she had changed. I was so hurt; when I needed her to be there for me, she abandoned me. I knew she had her own problems too (not that she talked to me about them), but the only thing I could think of was that she did want to talk to me about my eye problems, but, unfortunately, I wasn't emotionally strong enough at that time to do that. Maybe she needed to talk about it to help her, as we were close friends?

My other friends decided to be horrible too; they thought it funny to try and send me to the wrong lessons and said things to get rid of me hanging around them. I felt they were talking about me and laughing at me behind my back. I ended up totally isolated, spending my lunch breaks in the library on my own reading *Harry Potter*, and my confidence suffered further.

If you have a friend going through something traumatic in their life, don't turn your back on them when they need you most. Be their friend as you have always been. If they are not ready to talk about it to you yet, be there when they are ready to talk. I have real issues with self-confidence and socialising because of how my friends behaved toward me. It has taken me this long to rebuild my confidence, although I feel I have still a long way to go. It was so bad that I wouldn't go and buy myself a drink on holiday. Yes, pathetic, I know, but I would rather have gone without than have to get it myself.

I have put up this wall around me to protect myself from people hurting me. As a result of this, I know that sometimes I come across as being cold; I don't let people see the real Vicki until I know I can trust them. I lose all confidence when in a large group, as I feel that if I say something people will think me silly. I think my problem started when my right eye turned green and I knew people were staring at me.

In drama lessons at school we rehearsed little plays to perform to the class and I hated it, because I would think they'd be staring at my eye and laughing at me. I didn't lose that feeling when I got my prosthetic eye. One of the games we used to play in drama at school was 'Wink Murder'. Someone would be chosen to go out of the room whilst someone else was picked to be the murderer. The person would come back into the room and would have to guess who the murderer was. The murderer would wink at people around the room to murder them. I could never see who the murderer was winking at so I would decide that I had been winked at and lay on the floor. Yet another thing the teaching staff were insensitive about!

In English, for part of our GCSE module, we had to get up in front of the class and make a speech in pairs. I worried and worried about doing this until I felt really sick and screwed up inside. We were allowed to have notes to help us, but this was no help to me as I find it impossible to look up and down from notes to an audience due to focusing problems with my vision. As a result of this, I just read from my notes! I was hoping for a B in English, but in failing to engage the audience, I think my overall result suffered.

How I Got to Where I Am Now

I was sixteen when I started at Oaklands College to study Childcare. I suffered bad anxiety due to travelling to college on the bus; I was scared of missing the bus stop, and then crossing the main road to get to the college proved very hazardous! Dad had taken me on the bus a few times to get me used to the surroundings, but without him I had to rely on other students to get me safely across the road, as it was difficult for me to judge the speed of cars. I also used my monocular (like a binocular but designed for one eye) to see the bus number to check that I was flagging down the right bus. I had only been at college a few weeks when Mum, who is a practice nurse, had to leave home to look after my grandad in Abingdon, who was dying of cancer. I found myself living two different lives. The first half of the week I spent at home, going to college and work placement and the second half I spent in Abingdon with Mum. It was tough for the whole family not having Mum at home. I found it really hard and just drifted through college and work placement, not paying much attention to anything. I was in turmoil, as I wanted to be in Abingdon full-time to support Mum, to help and to be with Grandad, but to do that I would have had to give up college and I knew Grandad would not have wanted that. I was already missing one day a week to be there; I'd take my college work with me and study in Abingdon. Saying goodbye to Grandad each time was not easy, as I never knew if I would see him again, but when the end came, I was fortunate to be there with him. Grandad died in November 2006.

In January 2008 I joined another drama group called 'Fusion'. It was a professional group and quite strict. We had our own dance choreographer and singing coach. We were to perform *Peter Pan* and I was one of the Lost Boys. It required a lot of costume changes for the different scenes. I just loved being a part of the whole production, singing, dancing and acting, and it really boosted my confidence. We performed the first week of July, Wednesday through to Saturday in our local theatre, which included a full house for our Saturday afternoon performance.

You are probably wondering why I had the confidence to do drama outside of school but not at school? The answer being that they didn't know me, I was still the quiet Vicki, but they didn't know my problems, so I didn't feel judged. Strange, isn't it? Even I find it a bit warped!

The morning after my eighteenth birthday party, Mum was admitted to hospital with an overactive thyroid and she stayed in hospital for two days. That was a worrying time, as her thyroid kept on going over and underactive and there were several trips to the hospital.

In July 2008, I took a job doing relief work at a day nursery but had to give up drama as it clashed with my working hours. I stayed there for a year and a half, and hoped it would lead to a permanent position.

I started doing voluntary work in the village. I helped in the village shop once a week, which is run by volunteers from the village community. I really enjoyed the short time I helped there. I served on the till, did stock checks and unpacked deliveries. I even helped on Christmas Eve, when people came to collect their vegetables that they had ordered for their Christmas dinner!

I started helping at the Brownie pack in the village in 2005 and became a Young Leader. I was called Snowy Owl (reference to Harry Potter's pet owl, Hedwig). I really enjoyed being a Young Leader in the Brownie pack that I was part of when I was younger! I helped with badge work, craft activities and organising games. I stopped helping in 2009.

My work placement for the duration of my Health and Social Care course was in our village school. Once I had finished my course, I continued to help there once a week until I got a permanent job in 2010.

In January 2010 I applied for a job as a childminder's assistant. My luck changed for the better and I got the job.

Six months later, my employer said she was leaving the area and was transferring the business over to a friend. I was upset, as I had become quite settled there. My new boss was different; she wasn't fair at all and I felt rather exploited. I didn't even get a proper lunch break away from the children. I only stayed because it gave me a workplace to continue my Level 3 in Childcare, so that if a job came up at Moorfields, I could apply for it.

I would like to thank Ware College, where I did my Level 3 in Childcare, who did something that never happened all the way through my education. They provided me with a copy of the whole

Powerpoint presentation that was on the OHP during each session; something that school and Oaklands College could never grasp.

I started to do voluntary work at Moorfields one day a month on my day off. Then, in March 2012, a job came up at Moorfields... and I GOT IT! The strangest thing was that I had created a vision board of the things I wanted and had put a picture of the 'Friends of Moorfields' logo on the board, symbolising my dream of one day working there. I truly believed there would be a job for me after I finished my Level 3 course. Visualisation really does work – as it was Friends of Moorfields who would fund my position in A&E in Richard Desmond Children's Eye Centre.

The three best things that happened in 2012 were:

1. Getting my dream job at Moorfields.
2. Going on my dream holiday to Florida, visiting 'The Wizarding World of Harry Potter' and fulfilling my lifelong dream of swimming with the dolphins at Discovery Cove. That whole experience was absolutely AMAZING! It has to be one of the best days of my life, swimming with the dolphins; I just felt so safe with them. The most amazing part was being propelled across the lagoon by two dolphins each pushing one of my feet. I managed to lift up both my arms into the air as they pushed me.

3. As a family, we managed to get tickets for the London 2012 Paralympics in the Olympic Stadium. We saw the visually impaired race; everyone was asked to be silent when the race had started as they had to listen out for their trainer to guide them around the track. It was truly inspiring.

Ever since secondary school, whenever Dad has driven me to school, college, or to the train station and I've been feeling down, as I get out of the car, he always says to me, "*Nil desperandum*," which means 'don't despair', don't let them get you down. It is meant to put a smile on my face, and usually does. It has changed over the years to, "Don't let the Muggles get you down!"

The entry above is for my dad, because when he was reading through one of the drafts of my book, he said that he wasn't mentioned. So, here you are, Dad!

Where I Am Now

Despair of Vision

"Is it not enough,
For it to happen once,
Than to start on the other,
The one that gave me much less bother.
Floaters to annoy,
Flashing lights and blurriness too,
Any more to add to this annoyance of
vision,
Must not forget the pain that is on a
mission,

To add to the misery that is inside me deep.
Is it actually there?
I wonder in despair,
Or is there something more,
Something worse to fear?
The emotions that come with,
Are too raw to deal with,
The anger that bubbles, ready to fire,
The short temper ready to blow,
And the tears that continue to flow.
Who is this person? one stops to think,
'Cause this person is not I, I blink.
Feelings of despair conquer the soul,
How do I get out of this deep dark hole?
So alone with this rare disease,
That no one knows much about,
How do I ever become at ease,
With this unknown rare disease?
The uncertainty of the future plagues on
one's mind,

For what would one do if ever became blind?
Oh, stop all those negatives,
Jump forward, you positives,
We'll deal with those negatives should they ever arise.
Jump out of that dark hole,
And find yourself again,
For there is much fun to be had,
With laughter to help mend,
And that, I am sure, will help those negatives to bend."

By Vicki Griggs

"It is the unknown we fear when we look upon death and darkness, nothing more."
Professor Albus Dumbledore
(JK Rowling, 2005, p.529)

Towards the end of 2012, not long after I started working at Moorfields, I began having problems with my good left eye; something I never dreamed would happen. I had this light blocking my central vision and could only see things around the outside. If I looked at someone's face straight on, it would disappear; when reading and writing, words would disappear and I had to rely on Mum to read for me, which I found really hard to deal with as I love reading!

I couldn't read small print close up the way I'd always done. Even with normal print, I had to bring it close and strain to see the words around the blocked central vision. I had to stop reading books and ended up buying a Kindle so that I could enlarge the font to make it easier to read. I love the feel of a book in my hands and had always said I would not be taken in by this new technology, but it was either get a Kindle or not read at all. I did start getting audiobooks from the library, which also helped.

Everyday life became a struggle, as I couldn't see the simplest things: the correct date on my train ticket or the price of an item when shopping. Nor was I able to sit with the children and help them with their craft activities, which made working difficult too. I now understood what it meant to be severely sight impaired.

It turned out that the abnormal clump of blood vessels at the back of my left eye had leaked fluid into the retina wall, which was causing the blocked vision. When I had my vision tested I could only read the top letter with my glasses (I can't see anything on the chart without them), which absolutely broke my heart as I had always been able to get the fourth/fifth line and I did not know if I would ever get my vision back to what it was. To treat it, I had an injection of Avastin into the eye to reduce the fluid and shrink the blood vessels to try and deactivate them from leaking more.

I was told that I would need at least six Avastin injections in my left eye over a period of six months. If you had told me that, two years later, I would have had fourteen, I think I would have completely freaked out. It was a long and slow process but finally the light at the end of the tunnel was shining brighter. I am now able to read the third/fourth lines again on the vision chart.

As a result of having a phobia of needles, I had the treatments under sedation and that had really helped me to cope with them.

The sedative would have the same effect on me as a general anaesthetic did. I would start off in the day room on the ward before the injection and would come round in recovery with an oxygen mask on and the nurses trying to rouse me. When it came to being taken back to the ward and sliding onto the bed, they would have to help me because, as much as I tried, my legs were just too heavy to move myself over! I would take just as long coming round from the sedation as a GA. Don't worry, though, I just like being unique to the sedation, as everyone else who has sedation comes round far quicker than me and don't come back to the ward on a trolley!

The light would disappear a week or so after having treatment, but then reappear a few weeks later. The only thing that happened between the light disappearing and reappearing was that being out in the sun would make the light come back for an hour or so and then disappear again.

I tended to feel most vulnerable after my treatments and sometimes felt like giving up. I was often reluctant to go back to work and just wanted to hide away and stay at home, but I just had to push through it and carry on.

In 2013, I had two major scares. The first was in March when, suddenly, I had a shower of floaters appear in my eye like a cobweb effect. I was scared stiff. It turned out to be PVD (refer back to 'What Is Vision Impairment and FEVR'). Then, in May, during a review, my consultant, Miss Wickham, thought she'd discovered a retinal tear. She decided to have a proper look under general anaesthetic (as my eye was extra-sensitive to light) to determine what to do next. I was devastated I quite literally went to pieces.

The night before I had the EUA, I found comfort and strength in listening to the S Club 7 song 'Bring It All Back' again.

It was good news. Fortunately, it wasn't a retinal tear at all, it was just some of the tissue in the jelly part of the eye that had folded over. Although very much relieved by this outcome, it left me emotionally scarred. I continue to get agitated when I have a review approaching.

At reviews, I begin by seeing the nurse and having my vision and eye pressure checked. She also puts dilating drops into my eye to enlarge the pupil, so that, when I have the scan, they can get a better picture of what is happening at the back of my eye. The drops sting a bit at first, but it soon eases if I keep blinking. It's a bit like getting shampoo in your eyes!

Next, I have my scan. This always leaves me feeling dazed because of the light flash when they take the picture. I have to try very hard not to blink. The flash usually leaves me with pinky-blue vision for a minute.

After this, I go back to the clinic to see Miss Wickham for the results of the scan and examination of the back of my eye using the slit lamp. This involves having a bright light shone into my eye, which is sometimes painful as I fight to keep it open if it is feeling extra sensitive. Eventually I give a massive sigh of relief when told that all is good. Never taking anything for granted is a hard lesson that we have learnt.

Often people wonder why Mum and Dad both come with me for reviews and check ups. The reason is that, ever since I was a little girl, it has always been Mum, Dad and me that have gone together for reviews, treatments, operations, etc. It feels unlucky if we are not all there as, if there is bad news, at least we are all together.

When this all started some people said to me, "You're not still working, are you?" They seemed quite surprised, but what else was I supposed to do? It may have been a struggle at times, but if it hadn't been for my job, I would have gone insane. Work gave me some normality between treatments and reviews.

Some things have changed that I find hard to accept and that has made me feel exasperated, angry and upset. If I look at a certain shade of blue/purple against a green background, the blue/purple disappears, leaving me seeing just the green, although I can see the colours in my peripheral vision (around the edges). This also happens with a certain shade of yellow. I have these fixed floaters that move with the eye. All these things get me down and absolutely infuriate me at times.

I get big flashes of light to the right side of my vision. I thought that I was seeing these flashes of light due to the fluid, as I hadn't had them before the fluid had leaked, but it is in fact the abnormal blood vessels that are on the left side of my eye (it's like a mirror effect; the blood vessels are on the left, but I see the flashes on the right).

I can sometimes see blood vessels in my vision if I look at a bright light to the left side. People with normal vision train their brains to ignore seeing the blood vessels, but because I have had disturbance to my vision, my brain can't always ignore them.

An interesting fact:

Humans are born with the blood vessels in their eyes in front of the retina, so if you have any problems with those blood vessels, they are going to cause problems with your vision. Octopuses, on the other hand, are born with the blood vessels behind the retina in their eyes, so if they have any problems with their blood vessels it wouldn't affect their vision.

Also, I have problems with dim lighting. I have always liked brightly lit rooms and places where I can see things better. If I am in a dimly lit room, people's faces disappear, and reading is virtually impossible even when bringing it up close. Restaurants are a nightmare, as nearly all are dimly lit and I sometimes have to ask someone to read the menu for me. It is even difficult for me to see what I am eating. I now use the torch on my phone, so at least I can read the menu and see what I am eating.

I get this soreness and a feeling around my eye that it is bruised, like I've been punched. It tends to happen when I'm tired or have been somewhere that has dim lighting. My eye becomes puffy, making it difficult to open. It goes from mild to severe discomfort and I also get pain in my eye too. I feel it has held me back from doing things, like going out in the evenings, as I am always worried about it getting worse and spoiling things for me.

The pain I've been getting in my eye has been a mystery. I was afraid the pressure in my eye had increased due to the Avastin injections, but I had my pressure checked when I was in pain and it wasn't high. We thought it could be eye strain and tiredness, but Miss Wickham said it sounded too severe to be eye strain. I did have a bad case of dry eye and was advised to get drops, which helped a bit but didn't anywhere near touch the pain, so it wasn't dry eye. This continued for nearly a year.

It was when we were on holiday in America in 2014, travelling the Deep South, that the pain in my eye and head was occurring nearly every day and I was practically climbing the walls, as I didn't know what to do with myself. The only thing that tended to soothe it was to bury my face in a pillow and put pressure on the eye.

After the holiday I went back to work, but I was so distracted with the pain that my brain really wasn't in work mode and I felt I couldn't give 100% to my job. The pain had taken over my life and I wasn't sleeping. At times, I was going to bed in pain and waking up in pain, and painkillers weren't even touching it.

I had a review soon after we got back from America and told Miss Wickham how I had had enough of it. She suggested referring me to a neurologist for an MRI scan just to rule out anything horrible before treating the pain. At the mention of 'neurologist', my brain went into overdrive and scared the hell out of me. It was at that point I hit rock bottom. Everything I had been through had finally beaten me down and being referred to a neurologist for an MRI scan was the last straw. The energy I had been throwing into the battle up until now had left me. There was no fight left in me.

In August 2014, I went to my GP, who said she would arrange for the MRI scan as soon as possible to stop me worrying. She also told me to take a month off work. I was gutted and angry with myself for giving in and taking time off, as I saw it as a weakness. Mum said I was being too hard on myself and that most other people would have taken much more time off than I had over the past two years. I just felt I had let everyone down by giving in. In the meantime, my GP started me on Amitriptyline to help with the pain.

The MRI scan was set for the last week of August. I was so scared that on the day before, I had a complete meltdown. Mum didn't know what to do with me, I was in such a bad place. I was so full of anger and was taking it out on the family; I wasn't myself at all. I was really worrying about having the MRI scan, scared it would be too claustrophobic and scared of what it might show. I needn't have worried so much. I didn't feel claustrophobic at all. They put something over my head that had a square in the middle so I could see the ceiling of the scanner and gave me something to squeeze if I wanted to stop, so I felt in control of the situation. They were talking to me through the intercom to reassure me and telling me how long each scan would take. All through the scan I just couldn't relax, I was so tense and stiff. I was so relieved when it was all over and my mood completely changed. I think the Amitriptyline was helping my mood. That night, my GP rang with the results of the MRI scan and it was all clear. Thank God! The source of the pain was still a mystery, although it was most likely cluster headaches or migraines.

In September, I went back to work and managed to cope a lot better. I still have my ups and downs, but I think that is all part of my eye condition and something I just have to accept. I had my fourteenth treatment and was the calmest I've ever been. There was a bit of a mix up in the anaesthetic room where I had the cannular inserted but was then sent back to the ward until Miss Wickham was ready for me. Usually I would be getting really anxious, but this time I just kept calm. I was called back to the anaesthetic room, laid down… and

I don't remember anything else until waking up in recovery.

In October 2014, the neurologist gave me a thorough examination. He thought the pain was a mixture of cluster headaches, migraines and eye strain, and prescribed a nasal spray to be used whenever the pain started, but it didn't work.

Through the time of despair, I have wanted to turn negatives into positives and to focus all my energy on helping others with vision impairment and, if possible, to raise awareness by writing this book. Also, I am looking to set up an online support network called 'Vision-Lite' for the visually impaired. It's a secure forum-based website where people can share problems and experiences with others who suffer vision impairment or sight loss. I am currently trying to get funding for the website.

Once Vision-Lite is set up, you will be able to access it through the website www.visionlite.org.

Please send an email stating that you would like to be signed up for updates regarding the website to vision.lite@btinternet.com

In September 2013, Mum and I started ballroom dancing. 'Fit-Steps' is based on *Strictly Come Dancing* and we loved it, as the dances were choreographed by Ian Waite and Natalie Lowe from the show. Sadly, it ended in May 2014 due to lack of interest and support. Instead, I now drag Dad to table tennis club at the village school!

I had been told that, because my vision varies, it would be in my best interest not to learn to drive. Since further problems, I now know for sure that I will never be able to. It is something I feel angry about, as I long to drive. I will always have to rely on others (mainly my parents) to drive me around; a deprivation of my own independence as we live in a small village. I just wish that sometimes I could jump into a car and drive myself somewhere I wanted to go, on my own, without relying on others or having to use public transport. On the bright side, I am keeping an eye on the Google driverless cars... watch this space!

Things That I Have Found Difficult

Having a vision impairment and the difficulties I experienced at school has made it hard for me to trust others to guide me and not to lose me or go off and leave me on my own. When I was eight years old, my class went on a camping trip. A few of us went off to the toilets. I came out of the toilet to wash my hands and when I turned around, my friends had gone. I didn't know which way to go and couldn't see the signs to get me back to camp. I was wandering around on my own until some boys and their teacher found me.

I learned to play table tennis at the age of ten, so when I lost the vision in my right eye I had to adapt. My brother, Wayne, coached me until I started beating him. At the age of fourteen, a few months after I lost my right eye, we were on holiday and there was a table tennis competition for teenagers. I entered and made it all the way to the final, and believe me, there were some very competitive boys who were really good. In the final I was up against this boy who had his arm in a sling; little did he know that I had only one eye, so he was playing his serves one-handed and I was playing the game with one eye; and guess what? I won the tournament. I think he was gutted being beaten by a girl and thought it unfair, as he was playing one-handed.

I recently challenged both Mum and Dad to a table tennis rally, but with their right eyes closed and their left eyes open. Neither of them could hit the ball!

I love going to table tennis club. I play against people who are better than me, which makes me improve my skills. In a game of table tennis, you look for people's weak spots in order to win points. Some of them don't know that I am blind in my right eye (which is my weaker side) so they unknowingly play that to their advantage. I can lose vital points in a game because I am not always on target hitting the ball on my forehand (I am right-handed) but it has helped to make me stronger on that side too.

Where I sit in restaurants can be a problem, as they tend to serve on the right side, which is my blind side, and it often makes me jump if an arm suddenly appears in front of me, so I try to find a safe corner, preferably where I can see the waiter or waitress approaching the table.

On public transport, I like to sit on the right side with my blind side to the window so I can see what is going on around me, because if I have someone sit on my right side I cannot see what they are doing and they may do something that makes me jump.

On trains, the stations are usually on the right side, so I can see the station name by sitting on that side. If I sit on the left side, I haven't got a chance of seeing it and, if it's dark, I haven't got a chance either unless they announce it.

When walking with someone, I like them to be walking on my left side so that I can see them, otherwise I will keep walking into them and then keep looking to see where they are. Mum can't understand my thinking, because she always wants to protect me on my right blind side so that people don't barge into me.

I love swimming and was a real water baby when I was younger, but since I have had my prosthesis, I've become rather cautious, as I have to wear my goggles whilst in the water in case my prosthesis comes out and then I would be in trouble. When I have been to water parks I have had some problems, as they ask me not to wear goggles going down the water slides, but if I didn't wear them, it's possible the force of the water would make the prosthesis come out, so when they ask me to take off my goggles, I take them off, but when I am inside the slide I put them back on. Sssssssshhhhh… don't tell them.

I, like many commuters, got caught up in the disruption caused by 'Storm Doris' in February 2017. When I got to the station, I heard the announcement that no overground trains were running, so I had to get the underground train to

Kings Cross. When I got to Kings Cross, the station was crammed solid with people, as no trains were running from there either. I somehow managed to get through the sea of people to the ticket barriers that lead to the platforms that my train usually leaves from. The staff at Kings Cross are usually always kind and helpful to me, but on that day I did have a bit of trouble. I called a member of staff over and asked if there were any trains running, which there weren't. I told him that I am visually impaired (holding my white stick up) and was worried that when they announced the first train to leave the station the waiting crowd would all surge forward. He assured me that it would be done in a safe, controlled manner, as the transport police were there to help with crowd control. I must

Me at one year with squint

Me at five years old with my little
guinea pig called Pickle

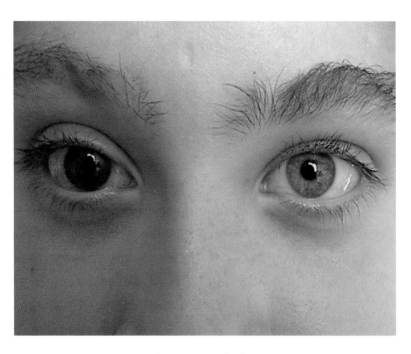

My eyes at the age of thirteen in 2003
(right eye green)

A signed photo from JK Rowling
(2004)

Receiving my year nine Form Tutor
Award from my Head of Year

1ˢᵀ Diploma

MARINA HOTELS

El Hotel Marina *Rey Don Jaime* is proud
to award this Diploma

to .... **VICKI** ....

for participating in the *TABLE TENNIS* competition.

23 of *Aug*, 200*4*   Entertainer

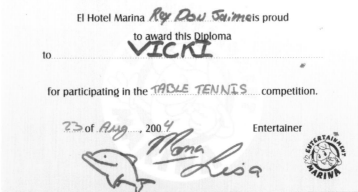

My winner's certificate for winning a
teenage table tennis competition on
holiday

With Bruce Forsyth at the BBC Studios
(2004)

At the opening of the Richard Desmond's Children's Eye Centre which the Queen opened in Feb 2007 with my Dad (Paul), Mum (Lynne) and my consultant Bill Aylward

With Rupert Grint (Ron Weasley) at the
vets in 2012

With Mum and Dad and our dolphin,
Dixie, at Discovery Cove, Orlando

At the Wizarding World of Harry Potter, Universal, Orlando

The Griggs family at the 2012
Paralympics

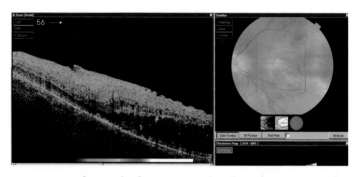

Scan of my left eye at the beginning of 2013

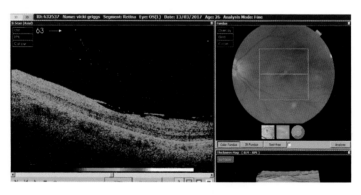

Scan of my left eye ,March 2017

Meeting S Club 7 at their 'Bring It All Back' concert at the o2 in 2015

With my baby Senegal parrot, Sunny

With my brother, Wayne

With my consultant, Louisa Wickham

Walking our dog Jessie over the fields

The wonderment of nature

admit that I was in a panic being in the middle of such a large crowd and, much to my disappointment, he left me there! I rang my mum on the verge of tears and she tried to calm me down, but without much success.

They announced the platform of the first train that would leave (which wasn't my train) and yes, I was right, there was a stampede, it wasn't controlled nor safe, as I overheard a woman behind me say, "I don't care who I push or hit; I am getting on that next train!"

They announced my train whilst I was still on the phone to Mum. I called over to the member of staff I had spoken to earlier asking him if he could let me through. Once I was through, he asked if I would be alright to get round to the platform. One of the transport police overheard this and said she would take me, taking my phone to speak to Mum to reassure her that she would get me safely onto the next train. Unfortunately, I couldn't board that train due to overcrowding and the policewoman was called to go back to crowd control. Before she went, she asked the train staff to ensure that I was helped safely onto the next train, which they did, and the added bonus was that I was put in the first-class carriage!

The January 2017 tube strike affected me as well. Tube strikes don't usually affect me, as I use the overground, but my train does go underground for its final four stops. It wasn't until I checked my National Rail app at 7am on that morning that I went into shock when I saw that all trains were being diverted to Kings Cross. I was completely freaking out by the time I finished reading it. I knew that if I went to Kings Cross there was no way that I could get to work. It would be overcrowded at the station and everyone would be trying to get taxis. I don't know the bus routes from there to work so that was out of the equation too. I couldn't walk as, again, I don't know the route by foot and its not safe for me to cross busy roads alone. All I could do was to ring work and speak to my line manager for advice on what to do. It was decided that I take unpaid leave on that day.

Subtitles used during a film or on a TV programme are another pet hate of mine! When wearing my glasses, I can normally see what is happening on the screen but am not able to read subtitles and have to resort to asking Mum to read them to me, which is equally frustrating for both of us. If there are too many, I have to resort to straining to try to read them or trying to guess by the body language as to what is being said! I would probably prefer not to watch anything with too many subtitles in it, so prior warning would always be appreciated.

Event venues such as concerts, etc. have no vision impaired friendly seats reserved near the front. Instead, vision impaired people are clubbed together with people with other disabilities, such as seats with wheelchair access, etc., which aren't near the stage at all but can be near the back. When I go to a concert, I want to be able to see what is happening on stage as much as I possibly can while I still have sight and can enjoy it. It was once mentioned to me in a conversation on this with someone that it doesn't matter where you sit at a concert; you are there to listen. I do agree with this to some extent, as I have accepted that I can't see and am happy to be a part of the crowd, but somehow that doesn't make not being able to see what is going on on stage any less distressing. Theatres are able to be vision impaired friendly, so why can't event venues?!

I am slow with my writing and need to concentrate, so if I am taking notes, by the time I write down a relevant point, I have missed what else is being said.

If I am trying to listen to what is being said and write at the same time, I lose the thought that I wanted to put down and leave myself with half a sentence, which is really frustrating!

This used to happen all the time at school.

How could I revise for exams with half sentences?!

By Mum helping me, of course!

One of the problems I have encountered with my own short-sightedness is: if I am in a room with a few other people and someone across the room asks a question without using a name, I often struggle to work out whether they are looking my way or not. It is only when no one else answers that I realise it must be me. In the meantime, there is a prolonged silence while I am trying to work it out, which is embarrassing, and of course they may think me rude for not responding. This is still a problem for me, especially when people don't use my name.

It's not just eye contact I miss. Mum and Dad are always saying things like, "Look! There's a woodpecker in that tree." They sometimes forget that I cannot see things far away and it's hard to know exactly what I am missing out on because I have no idea what a person with normal vision is actually seeing. I have taught myself not to care about what I am missing, but at times it can be very frustrating!

At primary school, sometimes I did not finish lunch at the same time as my friends, so I would spend a long time walking around the playing field looking for them. I would walk up to a group of people thinking they might be my friends, but it was only when I was right in front of them that I would realise my mistake.

The most annoying thing with having a vision problem for me personally is that I am a real daredevil; an 'adrenaline junkie'. I love going on all the fast rides at theme parks, although I don't feel it would be advisable for me to go on the daring rides like the loop-the-loops or any other rides that go upside down.

When I am on my own going to a shop that I am not that familiar with and am looking for something in particular, I can never find it. An example of this is when I went into Sports Direct looking for table tennis balls. I went round the shop three times before plucking up the courage to ask a member of staff where they were. They said, "They are over there," pointing across the shop where I had already looked. I went back over and had another look but still couldn't see them. I asked another member of staff and they said the same thing, so I had to admit that I am visually impaired and that I needed some help. It made me realise that I need to have my symbol cane at hand all the time, even when I am around shops in town.

I don't realise how much I depend on Mum when out and about. When I am with people that are not that aware of my needs, I have to fend for myself. An example of this is when we go to a party and there is a buffet. Mum is usually at hand to help me with the buffet, because I can't tell what food there is. At one party, I went up with one of our friends instead and, because Mum wasn't there, I had to try and work out myself what food there was and ended up with not very much on my plate as a result.

If I am on my own and I go and get something to eat, I always go to places I am familiar with and know what I want. If I go somewhere that I don't know what food they have, the boards are usually on the wall behind the till, which I can't see, and Mum isn't there to tell me. I find the whole situation rather embarrassing and it makes me feel insecure, so I try and avoid unfamiliar eating places.

I have heard a lot of children say that they are scared that they will need glasses because of being teased at school. This is so wrong. Where have children heard that it is not cool to wear glasses?

I have worn glasses since the age of four and started off wearing them all the time, but as I got further into school, I started not wanting to use them and only wore them during class. When I needed my glasses to help me find my friends at lunchtime, I suffered the consequences of not wearing them due to being teased. Children should not be made to feel like they are different from others because they need to wear glasses to help them see better. Those that tease others may one day need glasses themselves. It is nothing to be ashamed about, as it is not our fault if our eyesight is not like those that have perfect vision.

Levels of vision impairment can vary considerably from person to person. However, the general public often think that someone with a guide dog or white cane has absolutely no vision at all – this is not always the case.

I get people pushing in front of me when boarding a train to take the last remaining seat because they think that I can't see them doing it! When people do give up their seat for me, I then feel that I can't get my book/magazine or phone out because of their perception of a white cane meaning blind and worry what they would think of me if I started to read. It is very difficult at times living with an invisible disability. I use my cane in crowded places and places that I am not familiar with, so the use of the cane is not always consistent and sometimes I feel that people are judging me because they see me getting around okay without it and think that I have normal vision. They don't understand the reason I am using it.

Things I Have Found Useful

My National Rail app that I downloaded on to my phone has been a lifesaver to me. When there has been any disruption to train travel (train delays, cancellations, diversions, etc.), at times, it seems that the app knows more than the train staff! It tells you which platform the train is on even before the staff announce it. I always check this app before setting off for the station to make sure everything is running on time. The app lets you follow the train live if you keep refreshing the page, so if it is disrupted, I can decide to either get another train or wait. I can also check the app if I am unsure where I am or which station I have just left, to make sure I haven't missed my stop.

It is well worth downloading if you use the trains a lot; I certainly don't know what I would do without it!

BENEFITS THAT HELP

There are benefits that can help people who are vision impaired, which can help towards daily activities, etc.

They may be entitled to **DLA/PIP (Disability Living Allowance/Personal Independence Payment)**, which helps towards any extra costs that come with having a disability.

The entitlement to DLA/PIP will guarantee the entitlement to a **CEA card (Cinema Exhibitors' Association**

UK) that lets the carer go to the cinema with you for free.

You are also entitled to:

A **Disabled Railcard** to get a third off rail fares for you and a carer.

If you are registered with a visual impairment, then you can apply for:

A **free bus pass** to travel across your county for free or a **Freedom bus pass** if you live in London, which lets you travel across London for free.

You can get discounts for you and a carer to go to the theatre with seats in the front rows.

Also, many museums/exhibitions give discounts if you are vision impaired or have other disabilities.

I have found having a dictaphone at

hand when having to take notes really useful, as I can concentrate on listening to what is being said and take notes at my own pace later.

THE IMPORTANCE
OF EYE CHECKS

Having regular check ups with your optician is very important, to ensure that your eyes remain in good health and to identify any signs of vision loss. If you do have your vision checked regularly, then you will be aware of the vision chart called the Snellen test, used to measure the distance one can see. It is a chart with single letters that get smaller, line by line. Your Snellen score consists of two numbers. The first represents the distance from the chart from which you are able to read it. The second represents the distance for someone with normal vision. A Snellen score of 6/24 would mean that what you can read from six metres, a person with normal vision could read from twenty-four meters.

Nearly two million people in the UK are affected by low vision. The Low Vision Aid clinic is similar to the optician but also supplies aids to help with everyday life. They have equipped me with an LED magnifier and a small monocular.

Experiences Using a Symbol Cane

I have a white stick. Most people assume it means the person is blind, but that is not always the case. There are different kinds of white canes available depending on one's needs.

The shortest is called a symbol cane (although you can get different sizes of a symbol cane) designed only to alert people to your vision impairment. I own one of these.

The guide cane is longer than a symbol cane and is used as a mobility aid, which helps in avoiding obstacles and alerts you to pavement edges and kerbs.

The long cane is also used as a mobility aid, to scan the ground by sweeping the cane from side to side to detect obstacles, kerbs and pavement edges.

A white and red stick is to alert people that the person has vision and hearing impairment and can come as a symbol cane, guide cane or long cane.

A symbol cane does exactly as its name describes – it symbolises that you have a vision impairment or sight problem. The cool thing about a symbol cane is that it is foldable, so you can hide it up your sleeve when you don't need it. I use the symbol cane to alert people behind me that I can't see on my right side. I hold it out, slightly to the right, so that if I cut in front of them, they might make allowances. Also, it might make people think twice before cutting in front of me on that side and stop them from startling me.

It has taken me until quite recently to accept that I have a disability, because I have always tried to carry on as normally as possible and have not thought of my condition as a disability. As I have said before, I have gotten into some sticky situations because my condition is not visible – one in particular I have never forgotten. I was on a cruise holiday with my mum and dad and in the evenings, we often attended the shows they put on, but one night we had seats further back and I wasn't able to see as well. Mum spotted there were seats for the disabled at the front and told me to go and sit there. I wouldn't go on my own, so Mum joined me. An elderly couple came and sat next to us; the man was in a wheelchair and the woman said, "You realise these are disabled seats." I didn't say anything but leaned over to Mum and told her what the woman had said as I was upset. Mum leaned over to the woman and said, "Actually, she can't see out of one eye and has limited vision in the other." The woman then couldn't stop apologising to me. It just shows that you should never judge people, because you never know what might be wrong with them, whether it be visible or not.

Another thing that happened to me was when I was on my own travelling home from London. I had to get the tube to Kings Cross. When I got there, I must have taken a wrong turning as I ended up at St Pancras Station. I couldn't work out where I was. Then this man came up behind me and said, "Don't you watch where you are going?" I must have cut across him on my wrong side. "Actually, I can't see out of one eye," I replied. He muttered something under his breath. This is why I now use a symbol cane, because if people are not aware, they won't make allowances.

I have had some lovely people help me when they have seen I have a symbol cane. I was having trouble getting through the ticket barrier at the station, as the machine kept refusing to take my ticket. A man saw my symbol cane and said he would find someone to help. It was really crowded and he couldn't find anyone, but instead of leaving me, he said to go through with him on his ticket.

Another man very kindly helped me onto a crowded train, got me a seat when we had to change trains, asked me where I was going and said he would let me know when it was my stop.

On another occasion, my train was diverted to Kings Cross, where it was very crowded. Then the emergency alarm went off to evacuate the building. I didn't know what to do as I stood outside the station. A woman saw me standing there with my symbol cane and said she'd take me to a member of staff who would help me. I was in a bit of a state at this point as I was really late for work. When they re-opened the station, a member of staff escorted me to the tube and took me all the way to the ticket barrier at my stop.

It makes life so much easier when people are actually aware of my situation. They can be very kind and helpful when they see I have a symbol cane, but sometimes it can be quite dangerous too. If I am heading towards escalators/stairs and am concentrating on where I am going, when someone taps me on the arm on my blind side to ask if I need any help it startles me and makes me lose concentration on what I'm doing. I have had some near misses almost walking into things when I have been distracted.

Remember, there are lots of people with a vision problem who don't use a white cane because they consider it to be a private and personal matter that they don't want other people to know about.

Using a symbol cane has helped give me a bit more confidence in getting around busy stations on my own and helps to make me feel more secure in a crowded place (although I still feel most vulnerable and get in a panic if there is train disruption on my journey to and from work with overcrowding on trains, platforms and stations).

GUIDE DOGS

The 'Guide Dogs for the Blind Association' is a British charitable organisation which provides help to thousands of blind and partially sighted people across the UK through the provision of guide dogs. They also campaign for the rights of those with visual impairments and invest in eye disease research. One of the trips with SightLife was to the Guide Dog Training School in Essex. It was a lovely day out. We were taken around to see all the guide dog puppies.

A guide dog puppy is with its mother until it is eight weeks old. At around five weeks it is put through some simple tests to assess its potential for becoming a guide dog. It is then put with a family who teach the puppy basic training and commands. They take the puppy everywhere so that it gets used to its surroundings. At roughly fourteen months, the dog will move to a specialist trainer, where it will be trained for around six months to gain the skills it needs. This includes three to five weeks of intensive work with the new owner. Every person and dog is unique, so matching a guide dog to an owner is a complex process and trainers have to consider a person's walking speed, height and lifestyle.

Mum and I both decided to sponsor a guide dog puppy. When we received our packs, we found we had sponsored the same one, a rather special royal puppy, as he was named George after baby Prince George. George has become a qualified guide dog. We have followed two more guide dog puppies since George: Goldie and Buddy.

To find out more about sponsoring a guide dog, visit their website at: www. guidedogs.org.uk

Most people know that when you see someone with a guide dog not to touch or interfere, as this may affect their concentration. A guide dog is trained to stop and sit at every curb and it is the handler's responsibility to give the dog the instruction when to cross once they have listened for traffic and identified that it is safe to cross. If the road to cross is so busy that the handler is unable to make this decision alone, they will then drop the handle on the dog's harness and ask someone to assist them across.

Support Group

I never wanted a white stick, as it would draw attention to the fact that I have a vision problem and I didn't want people to know. However, when I began working in London, I encountered problems at train stations during rush hour, especially crossing over to reach the escalators. I realised a white stick might help, so when I went to my LVA (Low Vision Aid) clinic at Moorfields, they put me in touch with the Sensory Advisors in our area. The lady who came was very helpful. Not only did she equip me with a symbol cane, but also gave me some other gadgets that would help too; a Freedom Daylight Lamp and special TV glasses. She put me in touch with a support group called SightLife, and they really helped me through some very tough times. There were people there worse off then me and yet they were still able to get on with their lives and had a real sense of humour – we would spend most of the meetings laughing together. We teased each other as well, but always supported each other when needed. We had trips to the cinema, restaurants, bowling and crazy golf. It was real fun and a great laugh. It was like one big family, with everyone aware, to some degree, of what others were going through. It taught me that if the worst happens and I end up going blind, life still does go on and I will have to adapt accordingly. The group was a mixture of blind and partially sighted people. Those that were blind all said that they would rather be blind than deaf, and I think I agree with them.

One of the best things we did was 4x4 off-road driving in Suffolk. The most amazing experience for anyone like me, who can't drive and probably never will. One of the instructors sat next to me in the car, telling me what to do and which way to go. We did a bit of driving around a course, and then some off-road driving through muddy puddles, up and down hills and through narrow passages. That has to be one of the most amazing experiences I have had (apart from swimming with the dolphins). I have always wanted to know what it's like to drive. The only thing is… now I want to do it again!

COPING STRATEGIES

I have never wanted people to know about my vision impairment, because I didn't want them to feel sorry for me. I have learnt that if people don't know about my disability, they won't understand some of the things I do and that can lead to upset; they may think I'm being difficult when actually there is a reason for my actions. What I was most worried about was people feeling sorry for me, but I have realised that if I can talk about it in the most positive, confident way, then they will just accept that's who I am.

The most difficult thing is accepting something, whether it is the loss of a loved one or, as in my case, the loss of my sight. You grieve for both. Years down the line I feel that I should have accepted it, but sometimes, when I feel a bit low, it can still hit me just as hard as when it first happened, and I become angry and frustrated that I still feel like this.

Time is a healer; you don't forget what has happened or what you have lost, you just learn to deal with it.

> *"Understanding is the first step to acceptance, and only with acceptance can there be recovery."*
> **Professor Albus Dumbledore**
> *(JK Rowling, 2000, p.590)*

It's okay to have those down times and to feel that no one understands. No one does, unless they have been through the same thing or something similar. At some point in life we all come to understand pain, be it physical or emotional. Even though we're not alone, it doesn't stop us asking:

"Why me?"

"Why did this happen?"

These are questions that no one can answer, but I believe these experiences can only make us stronger. We all have a pathway in life and we can either sink or swim. Sink by feeling sorry for ourselves and giving up on life, or swim by making the most of what we have. I can't see out of one eye but I can see out of the other; I have my legs and feet to get me around; I have my arms and hands. I am lucky

to have a loving family, a lovely home…
my list could go on, but you get the idea.
So, whenever you feel like you are going
down a negative pathway, think of all the
things for which you are grateful. If that
doesn't work, put on some music or do
something you love doing. You have to
want to feel better; it takes perseverance
and determination to stay positive.

When my GP put me off work in the
summer of 2014, she told me to not to
sit at home doing nothing all the time
but to set myself small goals/tasks (e.g.
go out for a walk) to just ensure that I
was doing something small each day, as
I could have sunk deeper into myself.

Life has taught me to seize the moment,
to make the most of what we have right

now; so, grab every opportunity that comes your way, do not have any regrets. Think of the impossible and make it happen.

If you had told me ten years ago that I would be working at Moorfields as a 'Play Leader', I would have thought it impossible; the unconfident, scared little thing that I was back then would have had a fit at the thought of being responsible for a play area, talking to parents and travelling into London every day in rush hour on my own.

I believe I can do anything I put my mind to, so I made a list of goals I needed to accomplish in order to get *Vis-Ability* published.

Since I started work at Moorfields, I have overcome so many fears which once held me back. I have pushed myself out of my comfort zone and have challenged myself to do things which once I would have avoided. This has boosted my confidence and has helped me to push forward into new challenges so I can continue to grow.

> *"You sort of start thinking anything's possible if you've got enough nerve."*
>
> **Ginny Weasley**
> *(JK Rowling, 2003, p.577)*

POSITIVE THINKING

Perfect	**T**houghts
Optimistic	**H**ealthy
Support	**I**magination
Insightful	**N**ever Give Up
Time	**K**eeping busy
Improvement	**I**nspire
Visualisation	**N**oble
Energy	**G**oals

When I was off work with the pain, my brother, Wayne, took me to the lakes and we bought some duck feed and hired a rowing boat. Once before I had hired a rowing boat with one of my friends and we shared the rowing but found ourselves going round and round in circles before rowing into a bush. This time, Wayne did the rowing while I fed the ducks. We decided to see how many ducks we could persuade to follow us using the duck feed and managed to get thirteen at one time. I felt completely at peace so close to nature.

I had been saying to my mum for a while that I wanted to go to church, because Nick Vujicic (a man who has no arms and no legs, and is my inspiration) had turned to his faith and found peace in God, and I wanted to try it.

We went along to one of the family services in August 2014. A story was told about a woman who had brought her child to Jesus and asked him to heal the child. There were a few times during the service that I wanted to cry. At the end, I did break down; I just couldn't stop crying. Our vicar, Susannah, came over when she saw that I was upset and talked to us and said a prayer for me. There was something about being at church that made me feel safe and I think that was why I broke down; everything just came out. I was really embarrassed afterwards, though.

One of the distractions that really helped me, especially when I hit rock bottom, was my favourite comedian, Miranda Hart. Her sitcom *Miranda* has kept Mum and me laughing when we have really needed it. It doesn't matter how many times I see it, I still find it hilarious. Thank you, Miranda.

Wayne and I are very interested in positive thinking and we managed to get tickets to Tony Robbins' seminar *Unleash the Power Within* at the ExCel in London in 2015. It was one of the best investments I could have made for my personal development. I was rather worried about the pain in my eye causing me problems, but I was fine. We had late nights, little sleep, early mornings, virtually no breaks, grabbing a snack here and there, but still we were full of energy. We did a 'fire walk', which involved walking on hot coal, and I didn't even feel it as I walked across. From that weekend, my self-confidence hit a new level. Mum and Dad couldn't believe the change in me.

My pets have really helped me get through hard times. Taking the dogs on walks often helps me clear my head, and they make me laugh when they think that you have thrown the ball for them when you haven't and they go haring off after the invisible ball! They fall for it every time! When I have had a hard day there is nothing like having a dog hug from our Jessie.

My parrot, Sunny, has helped relax me through stressful times. When I get him out, he starts quacking with excitement, which always makes me laugh (no idea where he got the quacking from!). We sit together and I talk to him until he starts to flit his wings, which means he is wanting to relax. We both then sit quietly and nearly go to sleep.

Good Things Happen from the Bad

I shall never know the sort of life I might have led with normal vision, but I can only be grateful for all the wonderful things I have experienced, many of which only happened because of the difficulties I encountered; and perhaps I am more grateful than most for the things I do have. I certainly try to make the most of everything, because I never know when things might change.

It has inspired me to write my story and also to consider the possibility of talking in schools about my experiences. I truly believe that after everything I have been through, I am a stronger person because of it.

All my life, my parents have tried to make sure that I have lots of memories, special memories that I can always cherish, experiences that will stay with me forever. They have done this because we have learned through me having my eye problem that if we want to do something/experience something, we do it. They have ensured that if the worst happens and I go blind (note: no one can tell the future), at least I'll have all the memories of all the lovely things I have done and all of those special family memories too.

On our main holiday of 2016, we travelled across California and Arizona with 'Great Rail Journeys'. Our last stop was at Monterey and, on the last day, we went on a 'Whale Watch' at 'Monterey Bay'. I had very low expectations of seeing anything as, in general, I miss anything that is worth seeing. This being because by the time I try to find where I am supposed to be looking (which is usually in the wrong direction), it has disappeared, so I wasn't really that bothered about going on the trip.

How wrong could I have been?! We first saw lots of sea lions on the rocks just outside the bay, a few sea otters and a sunfish (a white flat fish). Then… we saw a whale! I actually saw a whale! I then grew more hopeful that I might see more. Although I was extremely happy seeing a whale, what I truly wanted to see was a wild dolphin. My dream was answered, but I didn't just see one dolphin; our boat was surrounded by around 450 dolphins playing alongside the boat! I was so overwhelmed that I had a stupid grin on my face and started crying with joy. It really is a wonderful world.

It didn't end there though. The crew had heard over the radio that a very rare sighting of a sperm whale had been made by an earlier tour group, so we sped over to where the last sighting had been and waited. The crew were so excited about this that it had rubbed off on everyone else aboard the boat. We all cheered when one of the crew spotted the sperm whale blowing water a little way away. As we got nearer, we saw it do a final fluke (a big dive where it lifts its tail right up) before it disappeared into the deep sea. The whole boat celebrated as we had all witnessed this; even I saw it! I managed to see all of these lovely creatures by using our friend's binoculars.

You can probably guess what one of my favourite highlights of the holiday was!

I am a massive *Harry Potter* fan. When my right eye was at its worst, I could do nothing but lie in bed and listen to *Harry Potter* audio tapes. Gradually, as I got better, I was able to watch the films over and over again. At the time, there were only two: *Philosopher's Stone* and *Chamber of Secrets*. I watched them so much that, sadly, I know virtually the whole dialogue start to finish. When I was strong enough, I re-read all the *Harry Potter* books up to *Order of the Phoenix*. *Half-Blood Prince* and *Deathly Hallows* had not yet been written.

Anyway, I was going to write to JK Rowling and tell her how much *Harry Potter* meant to me and how it had helped me through some very dark times, but I had never got around to doing it. One day, Mum picked me up from school and told me I had a letter waiting for me from someone in Edinburgh. I didn't know anyone in Edinburgh and was eager to get home to find out who it could be. As I opened it, I could see the words *Harry Potter* and soon realised that I had received a handwritten letter and signed photograph from JK Rowling. Mum had written to her when I was ill and had explained what I was going through. Well, I was on cloud nine for days. I had a letter and signed photo from my heroine!

We are massive *Strictly Come Dancing* fans and I was very privileged and very lucky to have the chance to go and see the show a handful of times at the BBC Studios and that is all thanks to Sir Bruce Forsyth. My dad worked with Bruce's daughter Julie in the '70s pop group Guys 'n' Dolls and they have remained close friends ever since.

I would just like to take this opportunity to remember Sir Bruce Forsyth, who passed away on 18th

August 2017. Thank you Bruce for all of your kindness to me over the years. You are a *Strictly* legend and are missed very much. RIP Brucie. Keeeeeep dancing!

When I was off school recovering from my operation, I received home tuition so I wouldn't fall behind with school work. At the end of year nine, there was an award ceremony and I was nominated for the 'Form Tutor Award' and was invited to attend. I really didn't want to go as I was terrified at the thought of getting up in front of everyone with my new prosthetic eye. However, Mum and Dad talked me into going. It wasn't until I got there, sat down and looked at the order of awards that I noticed I was down for the maths award as well. If I had known I was to get up twice, I would not have gone. I was mortified at the thought of having my picture taken with the award when I went up to collect it. Also, why was I put forward for the maths award when I hate maths and am rubbish at it? When it was my turn to get up, my legs were shaking like jelly, my hands had gone all clammy and I really didn't want to be there. When we got the pictures of me holding my awards, I looked completely terrified as I found it hard to smile with everyone watching me.

Something else that never would have happened if I had not been a patient at Moorfields Eye Hospital, was that Mr Aylward managed to get us an invitation to the opening of the 'Richard Desmond Children's Eye Centre' by Her Majesty the Queen in February 2007. We were not expecting to meet the Queen; just being there and being a part of it was enough, and when she arrived on our floor and we got our first glimpse of her, my heart was in my mouth and my legs turned to jelly as she walked past us and looked at me. The atmosphere was electric. Then, unexpectedly, we were invited to go over and to be introduced to Her Majesty. It was a very surreal few minutes. Mum did most of the talking and told her that it was my ambition to work at Moorfields as a play leader and the Queen said, "That's a marvellous idea." I had the Queen's approval! I did manage to speak as I was determined not to let this opportunity go without saying something, and so I said, "I am studying Childcare at college." One sentence, I know, but that was all I could manage.

We spoke to her for a few minutes and she showed a real interest in what we were saying and did not rush us.

Her Majesty spent forty-five minutes touring the new hospital before the official opening ceremony where she unveiled the plaque. It was amazing how precise the timing of everything was. Once finished on our floor, everyone streamed down the stairs and stopped on the first-floor landing, where there was a small window from which we could watch the ceremony. The whole experience was awesome!

I still can't believe that I am working at Moorfields, one of the best eye hospitals in the world. It was always my ambition to work there. My job requires empathy and understanding in dealing with the patients and their families and what they are going through. I talk through with the children what will happen if they need to have eye drops, scans, ultrasounds, or even MRI and CT scans. I know what it's like, because I have experienced all these things myself.

Sometimes I take my job for granted and get swept along with everyday life, but when a child in distress attends, it reminds me of why I wanted to work at Moorfields in the first place, to help the children and their families.

I try to make it as fun as possible: I plan craft activities, decorate the walls with children's pictures and posters, and have a special area where I put up a themed display. I often get comments from parents saying, "It's more like a nursery than a hospital," which I take as a big compliment. It shows how times have changed since I was a child patient there.

One thing I must mention is that something completely out of the ordinary happened when we took our dog, Holly, to the vets in 2012.

We were sat in the waiting area when these two people walked past. Mum started mouthing something at Dad and me, and then we realised what she was saying. One of the people who had walked past was Rupert Grint (Ron Weasley from *Harry Potter*)! The odds of this happening is so small, but this really did happen. He was there with his dad. Rupert had gone out to the car and his dad was there waiting. Mum went over to him and asked him, "Is that your son?

Is that Rupert Grint?" His dad went and called him back in so that I could have my picture taken with him in the middle of the vets! I was rather embarrassed. There was only one other person in the waiting area when this happened, and he was in hysterics watching us!

So, good things can happen from the bad; although you may not think it at the time, every cloud has got a silver lining!

My Inspirations

HARRY POTTER

Through the times of losing my right eye, when my grandad was dying of cancer and through each struggle, every twist and turn through my teens, I delved into a different world, a world that was very different from my own and where I could lose myself in the magic and adventures that became so real to me: the magical world of *Harry Potter*.

JK Rowling will never know how much *Harry Potter* helped me during the darkest times of my teens and I want to thank her, from the bottom of my heart, for giving us *Harry Potter*. When I was in pain, it was not just in my eye but all around my eye and in my head as well. In the *Harry Potter* books, the scar on Harry's forehead starts causing him pain too and I fully related to that.

I remain and always will be a massive fan and will always hold *Harry Potter* close to my heart.

> *"The stories we love best do live in us forever, so whether you come back by page or by the big screen, Hogwarts will always be there to welcome you home."*
>
> *JK Rowling*

I would like to take this opportunity to raise my wand in remembrance of Alan Rickman, who passed away on 14th January 2016. He played Professor Snape, the character we all loved to hate, in all eight *Harry Potter* movies. RIP Alan/*

'*Always.*'

Professor Snape
(JK Rowling, 2007, p.753)

* *Page three hundred and ninety-four (JK Rowling, 1999, p.128)*

Nick Vujicic

When I was at my lowest of lows, Dad found a clip of an inspirational speaker who was born with no arms and no legs. His name is Nick Vujicic. The first time I watched him, I cried, because here was a person that could understand my pain. He has no arms and no legs but is still able to swim, play football, skateboard, etc. How, you ask yourself, does he manage to do that? The answer is, by not giving up, and not letting his disability beat him, by trying over and over again until he succeeds. He is an inspiration to us all.

He has had to overcome so much that it made my problem seem so small. He inspired me to look at my situation in a different light and this gave me a boost which I really needed. He inspired me to consider speaking myself, to raise awareness of vision impairment and to write this book. In fact, it was actually when I sat down and started writing what to talk about that it turned into *Vis-Ability*.

When I heard that Nick was coming to the UK in May 2015 to talk at the ExCel in London, I was so excited, but then realised it would be when I was away on holiday. I was so upset as I had been longing for Nick to come to the UK. I am hoping he will return one day to talk some more, so that I can be there. To find out more about Nick and to purchase his books and DVDs, visit his websites:

www.nickvujicic.com
www.attitudeisaltitude.com

To see Nick in action on YouTube, type in 'Nick Vujicic'.

SPECIAL FRIENDS

One person who has stuck with me through everything is my best friend Natalie. We were at pre-school and primary school together but only became close friends when we both went to the same secondary school and were in the same form. She really helped me with my confidence and with her encouragement, I started to go to after-school clubs that she also went to. Unfortunately, she left the school at the end of year seven but has always stayed in touch with me. She has always been there and has supported me through all my struggles. Thank you, Natalie, for being such a good friend.

Another person that I am close to and look upon as family is my friend Janette. She has been like an aunt to me. Her children, Alice and James, are like my little sister and brother, as I have watched them both grow up. I grew really close to Janette when she let me do a child study on James for part of my Child Development GCSE when he was a year old and although I don't see them as often as I used to, I still have a close bond with James.

Moorfields Eye Hospital

My family and I hold Moorfields very close to our hearts, as I have been a patient there for more than twenty years; almost all my life. As I have grown up, and especially now I am working there, Moorfields has become my second home.

When I first became a patient at Moorfields, there were no special children's clinics and no play staff in the clinics that I went to and nothing for the children to do in the waiting areas. We sat in an adult's clinic with virtually no other children. I used to take a bag full of things to do and kneel on the floor, using the chair as my table. I enjoyed going to orthoptics, as they had some toys and a table to sit at. There was also a fish tank and two rocking horses, and sometimes they would bring down the Starlight TV from the children's ward and put on a movie.

The children's ward used to be on the third floor of the main hospital, and it is where I had many of my operations. The ward was quite small, but very friendly and cosy, and we got to know some of the nurses there. There was one small play room, another with baby cots, a kitchen area with a TV and a Sega computer game. I would ask if we could go up to the children's ward to see Sister Ero, because she would always give me a little bag of sweeties, but once I remember she told off my dad when he arrived late for one of my operations. We were so upset when we heard that she had passed away in 2002.

What the children have these days is amazing! A member of the play team on each of the four floors with toys, colouring and craft activities, a Nintendo Wii, and movies too. They can mix with other children who have similar conditions and strike up friendships with each other. Parents talk to each other too, as there is nothing like discussing your own experiences with someone who understands exactly what you are going through.

Mum and Dad have always been honest with me. Throughout my childhood, they never hid anything from me but tried, as best they could, to explain everything to me. I remember when I was six or seven and being upset about something I could not do because of my eyes. Mum said something about the abnormal clump of blood vessels in my left eye, which left me shocked and even more upset. I had not realised, or had forgotten, that I had the abnormal clump of blood vessels in my left eye too and it wasn't normal either, although we had always called it 'my good eye'.

I personally think that if you keep a child in the dark, it's likely they will have little trust in you or the medics when you need them to co-operate. I know parents are trying not to scare their child, but it could be more frightening if suddenly an operation is sprung upon them without any warning and they have no understanding of what is happening.

We cannot thank the staff at Moorfields enough for everything they have done for me, particularly Mr Bill Aylward, who was my consultant for eighteen years and Miss Louisa Wickham, who has taken over my care from Mr Aylward. We would also like to thank Sir Peng Khaw, who was treating my right eye when I was thirteen; also Nick and David in prosthetics, anaesthetist Nick and everyone else. THANK YOU!

Our family put on a New Year's Eve party from 2001–2017 for our village, which included a raffle to raise money for Moorfields Charity. People were very kind in donating prizes, and so to all our village friends that attended our parties and helped to raise money for Moorfields: THANK YOU!

Epilogue

My review appointment of March 2017 was one of the best reviews I have had. When we saw Miss Wickham, she looked at the scan and said, "It's amazing." The retina is now completely flat compared to when I had a bulge in the retinal wall. The exudate from where the fluid had been had completely gone! It is a complete miracle!

My review appointments have now been lengthened to six months.

Mum and I have a little ritual before going to bed. We have said affirmations every night since the fluid appeared and, who knows, they may have helped – we believe so.

The power of the mind really is the most powerful thing!

A NOTE FROM MUM

"One thing I have learnt from living my life with my daughter, Vicki, is to always try to look for the good in every situation. Good so often comes from bad.

We have had many special happy times together, which have given us lovely memories. We have always tried to live our lives to the full: wonderful holidays and days out, theatre and cinema trips, *family and friends' parties. We learnt to take one day at a time, especially when times were tough.*

I have always encouraged Vicki to have a purpose in life and am so proud of all her achievements thus far. I did work hard with her when she was younger, helping her as much as I could academically, always totally convinced that she would have so much to give if she could get into a position where she would be able to help others.

Due to her own life experiences (so far), Vicki has helped families in times of upset and stress in her work at RDCEC. As Vicki's mum, I know how distressing and helpless a parent can feel when their child is suffering – for us as a family, to have had someone like Vicki to talk to would have been so helpful and supportive.

All of Vicki's family are so proud of her achievements, especially in writing this book."

Lynne Griggs

My Message to You

In this book, I have talked about the education system and bullying. These are subjects I feel strongly about, because if my teachers and peers had fully understood my vision impairment and I had received the proper support, then my journey to this moment could have been a lot easier and I would have been a lot happier. I am wanting to promote this so that future generations of children who have a vision impairment, or any other disability, get the help and support they need.

The aim of this book is not only to raise awareness of vision impairment, but also to reach out to those who have a vision impairment. If this book helps just one person, then I have achieved my goal.

If you want to get in touch, please visit my website, www.vickigriggs.com, and send me an email.

To everyone out there, no matter what you have been through or what you are going through, be grateful for everything you have. Live each day as if it's your last; make the most of life, as you never know when things might change. If you see someone having a bad day, be the person to make them smile… remember that every cloud has got a silver lining…

And the most important thing is to just be you.

Love,

Vicki xx

"Mischief Managed."

Messrs Moony, Wormtail, Padfoot and Prongs

(Rowling, 1999, p.144)

Acknowledgements

Firstly, thanks to my family: to my **mum** for being my rock in life, to my **dad** for always being there for me and to my brother **Wayne** for your positive pep talks when I've been down.

A special thank you to those that have been involved in helping with my book, to the people who have been part of my focus group and who have given very useful and lovely feedback:

Natalie Wade, Janette Atkins, Anne Weekes, Jane Smythe, Rommie Swan, Hedda Campbell, Heather Parker,

Bill Aylward, **Louisa Wickham**, **Myra Charman** and **Shona Hyde**.

To **Sue Forster** at **Guide Dogs** and **RNIB** for their input.

Thanks to my best friend, **Natalie**, for sticking with me through everything and for keeping in touch when you moved away.

Thanks to my family friend, **Janette**, and her children, **Alice and James** (who are more like a younger sister and brother to me!).

Thanks to my godmother, **Myra**, for all her help and support towards the publication of this book.

Thanks to my two good friends, **Flossie Donovan** and **Suzie Ardeman**.

Flossie has always been so supportive throughout the last seven years and has always come to see me at Sedgwick Ward when I have had treatments (thanks Floss). Suzie is a Potterhead like me and never says no to going back to HP Studio Tour.

A very special thank you to two very important people for all their care over the years, my two consultants, **Bill Aylward** and **Louisa Wickham**.

A special thanks also goes to **Heather Parker**, who has been a lifesaver on more than one occasion.

Thanks to everyone I work with at the **RDCEC** for all of the kindness, support and understanding you showed me during my hard times, particularly:

Mally Scrutton, **Ann Houlston**, **Lauren Blackshaw**, **Chris Starr**, **Clare Price**, the rest of the **A&E Team** and the **Play Team**.

Thanks to all the staff at **Moorfields Eye Hospital** for all that you have done for me, particularly **James** on **Sedgewick Ward** and everyone else; you know who you are.

Thanks to **Vicky Palumbo** for founding SightLife, a group I don't know what I would have done without and to **Susannah Underwood**, our village vicar.

Thanks to **Miranda Hart**, for making me laugh when I hit rock bottom (don't know what I would have done without your sitcom!); to **Nick Vujicic**, for your inspirational video clips (you have really helped me to see my situation in a different light and inspired me to write this book); to **JK Rowling**, for all your kind letters that you sent to me and for writing *Harry Potter*; to the late

Sir Bruce Forsythe, for being so kind and generous with all the tickets for *Strictly*.

Thanks to the **train staff of First Capital Connect (Great Northern)** who work at Kings Cross Station, who have helped me.

Thanks again to everyone else whom I have mentioned in this book and to everyone whom I may have not mentioned that has helped and supported me through my life.

USEFUL RESOURCES

BOOKS

By Nick Vujicic
Life Without Limbs
Unstoppable
Limitless
Stand Strong

By Rhonda Byrne
The Secret
The Magic
The Power

There is also:
The Secret to Teen Power by Paul Harrington for teens 12+

By Paul McKenna
3 Things That Will Change Your Destiny Today
Instant Confidence

Other Books
Calm by Michael Acton Smith
Real Confidence by Psychologies
Big Magic by Elizabeth Gilbert

I have found that taking time for meditation and being mindful has helped me to clear my mind and to refocus on my goals. Affirmations and creating a vision board of my goals and things that I want helps to motivate me in working towards these goals.

MAGAZINES AND APPS
Breathe magazine
In the Moment magazine
Psychologies magazine
'Calm' app
'Headspace' app

The song 'Flowers of the Forest' by Mike Oldfield – *Feel Voyager*, that I downloaded from iTunes, is the song I use for six-minute meditation when I need that bit of extra courage to get through something difficult, or just need to shift my mood.

If this book has helped you and you would like to get in touch, I'd be happy to hear from you. Visit my website, **www.vickigriggs.com**, and send me an email.

References

(In Order of Appearance)

ROWLING, JK, *Harry Potter and the Philosopher's Stone*, London, Bloomsbury

ROWLING, JK, *Harry Potter and the Half-Blood Prince*, London, Bloomsbury

ROWLING, JK, *Harry Potter and the Goblet of Fire*, London, Bloomsbury

ROWLING, JK, *Harry Potter and the Order of the Phoenix*, London, Bloomsbury

ROWLING, JK, *Harry Potter and the Deathly Hallows*, London, Bloomsbury

ROWLING, JK, *Harry Potter and the Prisoner of Azkaban*, London, Bloomsbury

ROWLING, JK, *Harry Potter and the Prisoner of Azkaban*, London, Bloomsbury